Remembering the Body

Acknowledgements

Poems in this collection have previously appeared in: 13, Blue Rock Review, Concho River Review, Each Man has One Life (Trilobite Press), Front Range Review, MO: Writings from the River, New Formalist, New Texas, Penwood Review, Ruminate, Sincerely Elvis (Hot Biscuit Productions), Teacher's Voice, Texas Review, The Life of Ben and Other Poems (MA Thesis UNT), Travelin' Music: A Poetic Tribute to Woody Guthrie (Village Books Press, 2010), Windhover, & Windward Review.

Remembering the Body

Alan Berecka

MONGREL EMPIRE PRESS
NORMAN, OKLAHOMA, UNITED STATES OF AMERICA

Norman, Oklahoma, USA
2011

MONGREL EMPIRE PRESS
NORMAN, OK

ONLINE CATALOGUE: WWW.MONGRELEMPIRE.ORG

Founding Member

OKLAHOMA
SMALL PRESS
ASSOCIATION

This publisher is a proud member of

[clmp]

COUNCIL OF LITERARY MAGAZINES & PRESSES
w w w . c l m p . o r g

Book design by Mongrel Empire Press using iWork Pages.

To all of those who helped with the production of this book, especially Nathan Brown, Jerry Cobarruvias, and Jeanetta Mish, and to all of those who have guided its author, especially Alice, Rachael and Aaron.

Contents

Part 1
Body of Art

The Evolving Case for De-evolution

IV

My legs come from my grandfather—
a man who could stand up straight
and look a pygmy in the eye.
My arms come from his wife
an Amazon whose shadow
towered over their married life.

In Biology class, I studied that chart
with those many-postured sapiens
and worried that I might be the missing
cog in our genetic transmission
that would slam the ascent
of man into full reverse.

III

One spring night in Matamoros, I staggered
past some kid standing by the bridge. He asked,
Hey, mister, you want a lady? Tempted,
but with friends, I declined and moved on.
He yelled, *Hey, mister, you want my sister?*
No thanks, buddy. He screamed, *Hey mister,*
you want a monkey? I hauled ass for Brownsville.

II

The other day, I left the library
and walked across campus.
The childcare center had moved.
Where it had been, a science lab
now raises lizards in glass boxes.

I

My brother-in-law tells me
often, poems once rhymed.

The Body of Art: Creation Myth
For Leslie Palmer

Seated by his crib, Erato played her lyre
and whispered to him each night.
She held his hand and helped him trace
the alphabet. Before he crawled, he penned
his first sonnet cycle. Poetry given flesh,
he wore out Bics by the hour, but his mind
never went dry. Epics, ballads, odes, lyrics,
verses rhymed and free, poured forth,
but not without great cost, for with each
word set down he grew. Every metaphor
or apt simile meant he would gain
a fraction of an inch both up and out.

As the syndrome worsened, he paused twice,
once to allow doctors to run their tests
and then again to pose for Botero,
who came to paint the prodigy
as the exposed Adam leaving the Garden,
barely hidden behind a wanting leaf.

But, no man of art or science
ever connected his condition
and gift, so he wrote and grew.

The obese colossus kept creating
even after gravity fell subject to his craft.
At first he hovered—a living Thanksgiving
Parade balloon, tethered by editors
and booksellers, until he grew too large
for them to hold; he slipped into space,
became a satellite beaming down poetry
twenty-four/seven to the ignored channels
of small home dishes. Eventually, he folded
in on himself and slid deeper into space,

a tenth planet, where seekers of knowledge
came to explore the surface, hoping to mine
the truth, but they never reached the molten
core where a steady heart still beats
and new poems are still dreamt.

Joy: Memphis, Tennessee, July 1954

A solemn child
      slouching towards
            his corner store chores.

As waves began to fall
      in torrents, through thick
            heat and opened windows.

Down-beating down—one true
      voice tuned in/turned out
            by a chorus of cheap radios.

Electrifying,
      pelting him,
            until he busted

Open and free—
      shining. He danced,
            skipping crazy eights,

Baptized in delight, bathing
      in the glow, as the *Blue Moon*
            of Kentucky heralded the King.

Thoughts on "Body and Soul"

In honor of BH (Pete) Fairchild

And you swear it couldn't be done,
but there was Willie Mays running
full-tilt back into the Polo Grounds'
endless center field to make an over-
the-shoulder basket catch. Not done
he pirouetted like Nijinsky, let loose
like Zeus a white bolt that caught
some poor sap trying his best
to get back to first. And the whole
ball park rose thinking, *There's no way,*
while Say Hey doffed his cap and trotted in.

A machinist's son stuck in Kansas
escaped to his room and listened
to vinyl spinning jazz while he practiced
riffs on his tenor sax, honing his craft,
but never finding the art that hid
from him just beyond reasoned
thought in the secret of improvisation.

When Gretzky was in his prime,
he'd gain the zone with speed
and then do a button hook.
Play-by-play men often remarked,
*There's no way a man can think
that fast.* They'd slow down
the replay, trace the path
of the Great One's pass, show
how the puck left his tape,
how it saucered just over
a defenseman's stick, how it
found its way through a blur
of skates and legs, how it landed
in open ice, the perfect feed

to a streaking Coffey, sneaking
in from the opposite point,
who scored into the unguarded backdoor
of the net, as the goalie, bathing
in red light, still clung to the wrong pipe.

I just finished reading "Body and Soul"
for the hundredth time. The masterwork
of a onetime pipe fitter and failed jazzer.
And I'll be damned if I understand
how I can again land square in the middle
of these men's lives, how I got pulled
back onto the middle of that ball field
but this time it's not the Mick playing
the role of the blue-eyed bringer of truth,
it's Pete Fairchild staring down
this minor league poet, delivering
the harsh truth about the vast gap
between my talent and his genius.

The Texas Poet's Lariat
For Larry D. Thomas

Beethoven, always, Beethoven
filling his studio's air, seeping
past his sapphire eyes and deep
into an arid white flatland heat,
or pouring into the lazy Brazos
setting its waters into a red rage.

Through it all, the seated poet rocks,
smoking a teeth-clenched pipe
that burns a fragrant incense
at the altar of his art—his ruled
legal pad, on which his large
sure hand forges crystalline images—
each line a cord that he twists and braids
until he slowly ropes his reader in.

The Would-be Poet

He kept his desk drawers
full of beautiful pencils—
odd shades of green, red,
yellow and blue—graphite
wrapped in wood and rain-
bow. He kept them
from his childhood,
unsharpened with sharp-edged
erasers. They were stacked
with great care, bound
by rubber bands. He took
great pride in his collection.

He told me he wished
he could become a poet.

Philip Larkin at the Reference Desk

With the hint of an amphibian's grin
he sank deep into his toad-like day
bemused that even a paltry living
could be made by pointing the way
to water closets and drinking fountains.

Larkin marked his time behind an oaken
desk, near endless shelves, where ancient
voices covered in a shroud of dust, bound
in buckram and leather, whispered a faint
invitation to their forgotten primal song.

Each night the darkened library sat empty,
its keeper moved on past shared drink and food
to letters and poetry and then a deep sleep
where he dreamt that he heard his own crude
bass voice join the one true harmony,
until daybreak when he returned to be paid
to sit behind his desk and point the way.

Vollard Fails Caliban

Vollard was an agent who supplied remote artists.

Monsieur Vollard, the burning French
primitive beached in a sun's bleached heat
writes in boldly stroked ink. *Send me
more paint!* He pleads for tubes of white,
carmine lake, emerald green and ochres of red,
yellow and de Ru. He explains, *I must work;
my vision will devour paint, but not the terre-
verte you so blindly sent.* Vollard replies
with color-filled crates. Gauguin creates.

Monsieur Vollard, the abandoned son
of Sycorax writes. *Send me more words!
What can I do with these copular verbs,
this bare-framed language of my obedience
and my curse? I am a sterile, loveless
thing of darkness, only once embraced. Send
me the words with which I can express
the language of sleep and island-given dreams.
Then my art will drown all books. The sentence
of my birth will end.* Vollard replies
with word-filled crates. Caliban cracks the spine
of each volume of his new *OED* and consumes
each word, but the gap between his dreams
and pen remains unabridged.

In Defense of the Narrative
for Rick Sale

Slipping past the desk, at times
he would stand in our beer-filled places,
a welcomed guest—a fugitive
from ordered space. He volunteered
for battle in our war and fought
well at my side that one night
when two imagists argued that good
poetry did not tell a story but created
visions that intrigued more than meant.
They held their own through the first
few downed pitchers, but when we moved
to the pinball machine to defend our
Miss Bishop, we humbled them.

With each shot they evoked Pound,
swore in Chinese and sweated
faces in the Station Metro,
but how could they win,
piling up the bells and flashes,
not the points, not knowing the trick
to scoring well was putting
the shots together to clean a rack,
earning the bonus, ignoring
the lights and playing the game.

Composition

Like some high priest of language, I sit and guard
the silence as they scrawl. Left to right, line by line,
their persons fall to paper, fused and spliced
and not fully developed. I will read their written
confessions of ignorance, pass judgment
upon them, assign the proper penance, and pray
that these prescriptions will make them whole.

So like some high priest of language, I sit listening
to their ink and lead being dragged across paper.
I can hear the promise of the beauty of A's,
the creativity of B's. I hear a thousand voices
singing praise to all our greatness. I hear the love
of language. And I have been spoken to by saints,
but they have been so few that I have come to regard
my belief as fallen, my god as dying. And so I sit
like some high priest of language and protect the silence.

Gilligan's Gone Again

for Yucatan Rodriguez upon his retirement

With Mary Ann back in the heartland,
hitched to a hunk from the rescue ship,
with the Howell's sinking putts again
with their fellow elites, with Ginger's
back pinned again to a casting couch,
and with the Skipper retired to a home
for ancient mariners, Gilligan decided
to follow the Professor back to academia.

Once there, to everyone's surprise, scholars
found that the first mate had a knack,
and not just for bumbling. He had an idiot
savant's or at least a gifted fool's talent
for finding errors and editing written expressions.
He mastered English grammar and began to teach
freshmen who signed up in hopes of three hours
of credit in Composition but learned more
than they bargained for. They took to his natural
awkwardness and unconventional methods.
They began to search their dingy schedules
for his name until one fall when, to their distress,
it disappeared.

                    The Little Buddy just slipped
away, back into the uncharted, unmanned waters
of his youth, back into the palm-shaded
and swaying hammock that he rides
all day long, oblivious to clocks and calendars,
his untied shoe string snagged in the hammock's
weave. The canned laugh track cues to roll.

Rewriting a State Motto

I'm at work in Corpus doing
my time riding the reference desk,
when Sally, a co-worker, walks up
and begins to flit and chirp about
how she and her husband are going
to go bird-watching in New Jersey.

I can't stop laughing. I'm picturing
gutted neighborhoods in Newark.
I see pale men and women wearing
khaki shorts, black socks, binoculars
and pith helmets. I see them spying
on pigeons, pigeons on sidewalks
and in parks, pigeons sitting on stools,
pigeons on stools singing like Sopranos.
I see neon and the Bada-Bing, a blind
they enter to watch tits do their mating
dance and the occasional woodpecker
pop up. I'm thinking about odd ducks,
jail birds, dirty birds and flipped birds,
birds that hum because they're loons
and forgot the words. I'm wondering
what kind of saps and suckers could fall
for such a load of horse feathers.

I'm doubled-over, drying my eyes,
gasping for breath, when Sally,
who had flown the coop, returns
from her office armed to the beak
with brochures about Cape May.
She piles on the facts about nesting
habits and migration patterns until
I have to agree—Jersey is for the birds.

A Texan's Reply to Angela from Baltimore
'Tis new to thee.
   —Prospero

The cooing winter Texan
writes warmly in cool blue
how much she misses
the Texas she grew to love.

Well ma'am here's the news:
this time of year I miss it, too.

Your January moon
has blistered red
in the white heat
of August noons.

Buzzards bake
in tortured oaks
and hope death
will stumble by.

In this dry heat the earth
cracks wide, opens to eat
small pets and skinny kids
who fall deep into the heart
of Texas, oh my Texas.

Long since the last Winnebago
headed north, we remain, infected
by a mad bullheadedness,
the kind that draws lines
in sand, hunkers down
in lost causes and Alamos.

So partner, write your
poems of blue bonnets
and whooping cranes,
but summer up East
where a cooler sun reigns.

Next winter when flocks
of birders migrate through
the Trans-Pecos and down
into the Valley to perchance
catch flashes of mandarin
flitting along its tropical path,

I'll polish my Justins, tie
my bolo, and tilt my Stetson,
to welcome back cool days,
star-filled nights and magical
madrigals from one bright oriole.

My Bone of Contention with Roethke

I knew a woman lovely in her bones.

I know a woman lovely,
and, I mean lovely, in her flesh.
It hangs on her deep, like snow
on a January pine. In places she
seems more liquid than solid.
Think, axle-deep mud, and, Lord,
how I love to sink in those ruts,
sending ripples of movement
in every direction, while I hang on,
riding the waves, and she with her knees
and toes pointing at the saints,
arms around me like she's crawling
through the air, carrying me
somewhere better than fine.

Theodore, you can sing your praises
of your woman's fine bones, but
I'll be listening for the melody
of corduroy stretched tightly
across my love's thick thighs,
a lullaby that sets me to dreaming
about taking a dip in her singing flesh.
There will be time enough spent
with bones and dust, but until then
let me drown smothered
in my good mate's flesh.

Prayer Said While Igniting a Candle

For Jill Alexander Essbaum

Oh forbidden woman, poet of heaven,
prophet, sacred nymphomaniac
of my dreams, your psalms whet my desire
as you sing on your once pristine sheets
now stained with your black art and ink.
I kneel at the altar of your perfect body
of work and pray that yes, oh yes,
dear saint that your heat and flame
might spread and ease throbbing heads,
thaw cold shoulders, melt frozen hearts,
and burn away the litany of pettiness
that keeps us from our mortal mates.
Let this votive lit to your image illuminate
our shame for the thorn and weed that it is,
so we might come to understand the sacrament
of sex and the full love of God. Amen.

Desire

One breath, dead coals fired.
My life, one look, your face sparked
desire. Fan gently.

Questions of Economy—
King Kong (Early Porn Star) Meets Adam Smith

King Kong was an ape, a big ape
with an eye for the ladies
and a tool forty virgins
could ride to school.

King Kong was no dumb
mountain of fur. Remember
how he threw those men
off that log, down the crack
in Mother Earth? Remember
how he got on top the Empire
State Building without a map
or being taken for a ride?

So why, King Kong, did you fall
so hard for that furless female
who got lost in your unevolved
palm? Forget Dr. Ruth. Taken
to such brutal extremes,
size does matter. So why,

King Kong, after all these years,
do I not know who to pull
for: Fay Wray in her ripped
blouses and evening gowns
or you a primal king lost
in his unconsummated desires?

So why King Kong, am I so relieved
when the house lights return?
As I toss out my spent concessions,
I know Robert Armstrong was wrong.
Something much darker than beauty
killed King Kong, that capital ape.

The Trouble with Criticism

We murder to dissect.
                    —Wordsworth

So I'm reading Hoagland's
essay on juxtaposition
but since I'm lacking
critical sophistication,
I'm not getting much
out of it until he begins
to quote Apollinaire....
            I read...
                    Two Flares
                    rose explosions
                    Like two breasts unbound
                                I'm a college kid
                                in Dallas sitting in a dark
                                dank booth pumping
                                quarters into an endless
                                Super-Eight XXX loop,
                                so I can watch a grainy
                                woman arch her nude
                                back; her shoulder blades
                                touch as she rises
                                and falls and rises
                                from her pinned lover.
            I read on...
                    Raising their nipples insolently
                                I'm again a middle-
                                aged husband
                                up late and alone
                                channel surfing
                                pulled by a rip tide
                                to the enhanced women
                                of late night Cinemax.

21

But as I read...
HE KNOWS HOW TO LOVE
I am pinned
by heat and scent
beneath my lover.
The bulging veins
in her tilted neck
speak louder
than her moans
that she agrees.

And so do I
as I read...
what an epitaph

Hoagland returns
to the text and now
explains that in the French
the quoted stanza,
which I have lived,
contains no verbs.

I'm standing bar-side
swilling flat draft beer
when this Raquel- Welch
in-her-prime look-alike
begins fingering her flesh-
filled décolletage. She flashes
a killer smile and winks
in my direction. Stunned
I return her attention.
But she shakes her
head *no* and points
behind me to some stud
in a tailored suit
who has a red rose
pinned to his lapel.

22

Oh, Stella Look What They've Done

Stumbling toward coffee and beignets,
through a brain-bound pounding louder
than Kowalski's howl, the hung-over
residue of a spring break night spent
looking for properly easy belles
but settling for jazz at two drinks per set,
swilling quart-sized milk carton beers
near the Court of Two Sisters, downing
hurricanes served in collectable glasses
and temporarily going blind while listening
to ancients play Dixieland in Preservation Hall,

I begin obsessing over
the money I poured down
the drain and try to calculate
exactly how many brain cells I pissed
into a now much mightier Mississippi,

as a nondescript city bus
breaks the trance, horns me
back to this unsteady curb;
over the husky driver, I watch
a route card flip as in a loud
foul cloud of diesel exhaust,
the bus named Desire rolls off.

For the first time this morning,
I know something real has been lost.

Honky Tonk Voyeur

The babe who brought the beer
was blonde. Her naked thighs
painted in faded denim
pumped beneath her as she moved
from booth to art deco booth.

His eyes followed her
through the smoke over the rim
of his once-frozen mug,
his fourth or was it the fifth.
He forgot his age and wife.
He imagined the impossible
and her hidden flesh over which
her pink sweatshirt flowed. Her motion
created a strong current that pulled
him under, set him awhirl. Hypnotized,
he eyed her in his cavalier way
noting every flow and sway,
until from across the bar she flashed
him a youthful gap-toothed grin.

Was it the beer, his lust, his ring
or the near-to-kindly smile
she sent his way that made him
blush? Flustered he drank up,
tipped big and staggered out.

A Minimal Love Sonnet

He
said,
The
bed.
Her
eyes
sur-
prised
flashed
feminine
wrath.
Passion
refused,
he boozed.

Life of a Call Girl

Maybelle the call girl from Ma Bell
called herself that as she worked in a room
with no windows, the trained voice with a smile
for her exchange. She knew her numbers
and by more than their names. They welcomed her.

Maybelle was told by her boss long before
she had learned her first area code by heart
that she had found her calling and had married
her job—it was the only marriage
a woman like her would be allowed.

All careers end. Maybelle, like most call girls,
did not age well. One night past all her youth
her switchboard was computerized; her dial
became a keypad; her gentility was lost to average
work time. Her concern gave way to quotas.

Maybelle's final call with Ma Bell began
when Juan Roca, who spoke no English
and wished to call Guanajuato collect
from the pay phone where he stood, came
into her position. She did not know
that her group leader, the boss's spy,
was listening. It would not have mattered.

Maybelle, the once consummate employee,
a few years shy of her golden anniversary,
had fallen behind. Minutes past the twenty-six
second limit with Juan, while seated deep in a city
she no longer knew, she lost it all. Trapped
in an electronic nightmare of excited atoms
she began to scream, *What is-o yo name-o?*
again and again and then, *You dumb ass
don't you even speak Mexican?*

TSPS Operator Thirteen
of the Voyager unit in Dallas, Texas
twelve stories up from the corner
of Haskell and Bryan was terminated
for falling production and acts
unbefitting a professional.

These days Maybelle, the call girl from Ma Bell,
gives her pension check to the nursing home.
In return they let her volunteer
two days a week at the switchboard
where she knows whose child or grandchild
is calling for what extension as soon as she
hears the incoming voice. They marvel at her
memory, as she remembers her honeymoon night.

The Assimilation of Vitas Perkunas

Passing gas was once the stuff of low art.
Back when the Litvoks came to work
in American mills in droves, a man was known
in his neighborhood by his word, in the street
by his handshake, and in the tavern by his fart.

When I was young, the old-timers talked
for hours about the greats—the hall of famers
of flatulence, the Babe Ruth of whom
was Vitas Perkunas. The Bombino seldom
looked one in the eye; he had a grip that any
milkmaid could crush, but the man could fart
like a foghorn mated to a machine gun.
And smell—his performances never failed
to bring a tear. When he bellied up his small
frame, preloaded with beans and cabbage,
to the bar, the crowd would grow silent.
He never disappointed. Like the young Ruth
toeing the rubber, Perkunas would swing
his right leg skyward, effort etched on his face,
then deliver. The crowd would go crazy
and scream *Gerai!* Vitas would refuel
on beer, bought for him by his fans,
and the tavern's free pickled eggs.

Careers end though. Even Ruth lost
his swat, but the Babe knew it was coming.
Perkunas lost it all at once. The end came
as he strained for a third encore. He stepped
into his delivery, but it wasn't there.
Something else was. He doubled over
in shame. His name, amongst other things,
had been soiled beyond repair. He sprinted
home and beat his wife. Her cooking no doubt
was to blame. He knew he was right until the cops

came, called by the landlady downstairs.
Weeks later the married couple reunited.
Vitas stayed at home nights. The tavern
got a radio. The men played pinochle, ate peanuts
and learned about baseball—an American game.

The Mad Cow's Disease

My Aunt Helen Puch, an old milk maid,
was an ugly ancient woman, big-boned,
large-nosed, who spoke three languages:
Polish, English, and, at times, Bovine.

Before forced visits to my grandmother's
run-down farm, my mother would explain
how her sister had *lost* herself. My father
would reply, *Too bad she can't lose
the whole damn herd*. My sister and I
would theorize that our Aunt Helen
had only been severely dazed by Dorothy's
house when it crashed into Oz.

Condemned by genetics, we would go and sit
by an iron stove, behind a metal and Formica
table, where the returning Puch women
conversed in Polish, while my wicked aunt
mooed and lowed and chewed her food twice.

When Helen finally did return to her
right mind, she found her lonely life
which she filled with the tabloids
that she memorized as she rocked
on her rotting front porch.

Some family members will tell you
that my aunt's sanity went to pasture
because she envied the care that her
drunken and distant father had shown
his milk cows twice daily. I believe
that her mind's return was prompted
by her knowledge of what happened
to dry Holsteins. For as my father
always said, *That old Polish heifer
might be crazy, but she ain't dumb.*

McDemption

Against my doctor-ordered, low-fat,
low-sodium diet, I sat choking down
a Quarter Pounder Extra Value Meal
as a bag lady returned her fries a second time.
She stuttered her anger at a zit-speckled kid
until a manager arrived to stand behind
the counter. The summoned man searched
for meaning in her barrage of spit and phonemes.
He apologized and explained that he wasn't sure
what she was getting at. Agitated even more,
she tried to reply but got stuck on the letter *b*
for so long that I thought she might break
into a doo-wop song. Finally, she said, *B-b-*
browner. I watched the man's face. I expected
him to say, *Look, lady this ain't the Ritz;*
it's a freaking McDonald's. But instead
he took the fries and said, *Let me see*
what I can do. As he walked away, she grinned.
And maybe it was all the salt I had ingested,
but I swear the whole place got a little brighter.

The Prophet

I'm watching a documentary
about how Armstrong and Aldrin
landed on the moon. It's beaming
down to my small satellite dish
and showing on my high-def TV.

I remember that day. My family gathered
at Uncle Ben and Aunt Fay's house.
He was a spot welder by trade. She soldered
for GE and got good deals on the company's TV's.
She always had the best set. We all wanted to see
history in color, so we sat in their den,
saw black and white moon dust get kicked up,
and heard, *The Eagle has landed,* all except for Ben.
He hid in his cellar, mumbling the rosary,
washing down his prayers with swigs of Wild Turkey.

My uncle dropped out of school
by the fourth grade, but he knew
that on certain afternoons the moon
hung in the sky like a powder-blue
bowling ball—the kind women use.
It didn't take a genius to figure out
that if a ball sat balanced in the sky
and an eagle landed on it, then the ball
would fall from its perch and set
the heavens to humming as tons of Ebonite
hooked toward the one-three pocket
of the Mohawk Valley. He prayed
the cellar would keep him safe.

His father-in-law had sized Ben up
years earlier, nicknamed him *The Idiot
in Search of a Village*, so no one tried,
not even his wife, to sober him or to talk
him up the stairs. The next day he dealt
with a hard hangover, and stooped a bit
as he shouldered a fresh load of ridicule.

The program I'm watching fades to an ad.
It shows a production line where robots
spot weld cars, and I begin to think
that my uncle might have been right.

The Fall Game

In the front yard, wearing a plastic Giants
helmet with its leather chin strap snapped
tight and my handed-down Jimmy Brown jersey,
I spent autumn afternoons playing one-man tackle
football. Not an easy game. The goal was to throw
and catch a pass without stepping on a fallen leaf,
which once tread upon morphed into Dick Butkus
or Sam Huff. Awakened, these man-monsters would fling
me hard to the soft ground. Covered in grass stains,
mud, and sweat, I drove to pay dirt. An ancient birch
marked the end zone, in front of which stood the Fearsome
Foursome, a chest-deep pile of angry maple leaves
playing goal line defense. I tried to dive or plow
headfirst to six points. Fran Tarkington
to Homer Jones—the Giants might win this one.

Neither my father turning into the driveway
from a day under a welding hood to find
his piled leaves strewn, nor my mother up
from the cellar and her endless piles of laundry
shared my optimism for Big Blue. They only
looked forward to snow and the end of the season.

Departures

The entire extended family went out
to the county airport that winter's day
when my uncle left on his trip to Florida
with his wife and son, an exotic idea
to my ground-bound, blue-collared clan.
We watched them climb the rolling staircase
to enter a deep blue Eastern Air
double-prop plane while we stood
behind a cold pane of glass, waving.
As the aircraft took off and climbed,
we waved even harder at our Lithuanian
cosmonauts. In the corner of my eye,
I caught my reflection waving back
as the plane banked from view.

Prerequisites
for Aaron

I played whiffle ball, tossed
a leather pigskin around the yard.
My son goes off to college
having quarterbacked the Texans
to the Super Bowl. He floored
Marciano with a left cross,
used his uppercut to deck Ali.
He jammed with The Beatles
and fronted his band The Rapture
on its world tour. He stormed
the beaches at Normandy and Anzio,
helped his friends James Bond
and Indiana Jones complete a mission
or two. He conquered Alexander
the Great and vanquished the Huns.
He explored unmapped galaxies,
teamed with aliens, destroyed
civilizations and ruled the universe.
He has even died and come back
to life ten thousand times,
so acing his Intro to Psych class
or asking a co-ed in burnt orange
out on a date should be a cinch,
as his X-Box sits idle and gathers dust.

Why Snow Birds Don't Fly

Heading south, I'm blocked
behind a creeping Winnebago
sporting Wisconsin plates.
He refuses to take the ample
shoulder, the way rural Texans
do to allow the fast to pass.
Rather, this snow dodo has me
broiling halfway between Cuero
and Goliad. Finally, I catch
a break—a long straightaway
free of northbound traffic. I gun
my Vibe, pull out to pass
this landed houseboat. As I attempt
to accelerate, I shoot a glance up
and see a gaunt, white-knuckled,
blue-lipped driver staring straight
ahead, down a shortening road.

Faith

I can get you now, said an elderly
barber. He was new to Cosmo's,
an old three-chair shop I frequent
when a disappearing collar
tells me it's time to return
and get my quarterly crew cut.
I looked over at my normal cutter.
In front of him sat three men,
unkempt and bored. Halfway
to an hour wait, I turned.

My cut in mind—clippers back
to the hairline, a number four
guide on the top, a number three
on the sides—I figured, *Why not?*
It wasn't until those words fell
from my mouth, that I noticed
the man's right hand. It folded
oddly back onto itself while it
twitched at his hip dancing
to a silent and spasmodic beat.

His back turned to me,
we headed to his station.
I thought about running,
about Johnny Depp roles—
Scissorhands and Todd.
I said a quick prayer
in hopes that he might
be left-handed, then stepped
up and sat in his chair.
He draped me. I gave him
the formula. He fired up
the clippers. They danced
in his cramped hand—a dowser's

rod honing in on blood. As the hum
neared my head, I pictured a tomato
falling into a Cuisinart. The clippers
landed hard on my skull. I learned
he used friction to steady his hand.

We attempted some small talk.
I told him where I worked, where I lived.
His clippers massaged my thoughts—
a buzzing planchette inching across
a cranial Ouija board. It asked, *Scalp*—
noun or verb? Then answered, *Yes.*
My hair fell in clumps onto my lap.
Finally, he stood in front of me
with a large mirror that he steadied
on his chest, so I might inspect
his handiwork. I counted ears.
When I reached two, I paid up,
tipped big, and bolted out.

That night I brushed my teeth
and took the first good look
at the shaky barber's craft. I found
the same cut I had worn for years—
even and without error. The thought
Should I return seeded itself
deep beneath my clipped hair
in a field of shallow doubts.

Belief

Although he is half-blind and knows
he shouldn't drive, my ancient father
limps his rusting van to the Nice 'n Easy,
his New York Lottery play slip in hand.

My life is spent waiting as plastic balls
crash around like bumper cars, denting
the inside of my skull. Each orb a phrase
or image, each a fragment of some poem
left unwritten. I hold on to my ticket
waiting for the machine to spit out
a winning combination, but today
all that pops out is an old punch line—
You idiot! I said bring me ping pong
not King Kong's balls! Followed
by the line from *Cool Hand Luke*
that Strother Martin drawled, *What we*
have here is a failure to communicate.
Followed by Porky the Pig stammering,
Th-th-th-that's all Folks!

I suppose we all know that the odds
of enjoying a happy ending are beyond
long, yet my father keeps playing
the same numbers that have failed him
weekly for forty years and his son
continues to waste barrels of ink, each of us
hoping for a providence that still percolates.

The Limits of Friendship

Lynn, a circus bear of a man, asked
me to teach him the game of golf,
so I took him to the driving range,
handed him a short iron, showed him
the grip and stance. I tried to explain
the arc of the swing. Then I teed up
a ball and stepped back. He swung
and missed. Slowly, he progressed
to scalding out worm-burners. I told him
to relax, that all golfers begin by playing
croquet on a grand scale, but his frustration
grew. In his anger, he muscled up,
brought back the club so hard he knocked
himself off-kilter. As he reached the top
of his back swing, he tried to pivot
while standing on just one leg. I watched
amazed, as like the Golden Bear trying
to free himself from a steel-jawed trap,
he buried the blade of my eight iron
deep into his left shin. He dropped hard
and rolled. He ended up sprawled
between the guide ropes, blood oozing
through his white sock. I had no idea
of what to say or do until he looked up
through the pain welling in his eyes
and asked, *Does this happen all the time?*
I hope someday he'll forgive my laughter.

Pilgrim to Shiprock

That awful Power rose from the mind's abyss.
—Wordsworth

Will you look at that. She half-
gasps, half-breathes—entreating
me to take my eyes from the road
as we drive through this land so barren
that no one has ever tried to run
the Navaho from it. I glance past
her and onto the bound horizon.
There from the wings enters a square
monolith, a mountain playing the role
of a beached ship. So distant,
so vast, but *how* distant?

The horizon melts. Unfixed, all nouns
come to life, joining a disjointed
dance; the road cuts in, tilting,
gyrating, seducing me into a troubled
pleasure. *Look at that!* Now commanded,
but I dare not. I stare only at the resettling
road. *Look!* I defy her order and steer
clear of the flux. I am no sailor
and need solid ground beneath me.

Bent on speed, we travel in thick silence.
As the road veers toward the native rock,
we close in. It can no longer be ignored.
The miles traveled afford me the gift
of gained perspective. Now constant,
the great stone offers me, a reluctant
pilgrim, a sense of grounded wonder.

Digesting Statistics

As I drive on I-35 South just north of West, Texas returning
home from a sparsely attended three-day reading tour, passing
the miles listening to Bob Edwards anchor the NPR news for one
last time, I snap to attention when he soberly intones a heart-
breaking factoid; news this bad is never easily taken. European
researchers have found that poets die younger than their brethren
who write in prose. Not knowing why this might be true, the
scientists presume that poets lead darker

and more tortured lives.

An upcoming bridge,
I fight its gravity
and the sudden impulse
to swerve headlong into
a concrete abutment.

I decide to exit
for a Czech breakfast.

I buy three fresh cheese
and sausage kolaches.

So much for statistics.

Voila!

"..."

—Marcel Marceau

Like Houdini,
he knew the risk.
There would come
a time when he
would not escape
that invisible box,
the one cynics
said was never
there, but he
knew better—
felt the cube
closing in,
until it
collapsed
in on him,
and he
and the box
disappeared.

Home for the Holidays

In large mindless herds, recklessly speeding,
forgetting lessons won, heeding poor instincts
at great costs, we, the prodigal lemmings,
find ourselves jetting back, to revisit the cliffs
with our baggage to exchange season's greetings,

to be rebound by bonds that we once escaped.
Some left through dumb luck, others left through
the clever use of retro-rockets engineered to brake
falling weight, some evolved mutant parachutes,
but we all landed on our feet miles from our fate.

Yet, each year we fall back into step, bearing
our gifts, as we drag reluctant mates and kids
back past the blood-stained crags, not caring
about their fears. Like Pandora, we will unlid
well-wrapped boxes and chests, as if daring
genetics and the past to bring their worst,
because hope always remains like a curse.

Part 2
Remembering the Body

American Orpheus

Before he left, they warned
him—the rules are different
down there. Not a single
glance back or one mundane
gesture. A certain shade
of beauty must be ignored.

Emmett Till, keep them eyes
planted squarely on the ground.

And for his slight indiscretion
he was beaten past the debt
he did not owe, past his youth,
past blackness, past all
suffering into the object
of a modern Passion,
an icon hung on yet
another wall.

Hypatia's Death

With her, fell Greece; fell the intellectual world. . .
—*Mangasar Magurditch Mangasarian*

Black-robed desert monks
trailing dust, following
a bishop's command
circled Alexandria—
a murder of crows—
seeking Hypatia,
chaste daughter,
philosopher, scientist—
last heir of ancient Greece.

Her day at the academy
over, she drove
her chariot homeward.

A sea of monks blocked
her path, a dark tide. It rose—
swelled around her chariot—
pulled her under, stripped
her bare. The strong
undertow pulled her,
dragged her into a church,
then pinned her to the stone
altar floor where honed
shells and a mob's madness
razed her flesh. Flayed,
she bled deep hot pools
in which the hems
of the black robes bathed.

Remembering the Body

I think I might convert, become a modern pagan.
The Baltic Perkunas, god of thunder, blesser
of sacred oaks, stern god of my ancestors,
holds a certain ethnic charm. But, I believe
if I stray, I would stagger into the sodden flock
of Bacchus. I could happily attend even semiweekly
celebrations of his ecstatic and orgiastic rites.

Imagine a religion founded in the senses.
What sins could its believers commit?
Father, forgive me for I have remained
chaste and sober for too long. What guilt
could therapists dredge up from the psyches
of humans left alone to enjoy being human?

But when I search my local *Yellow Pages*
for Bacchean Temples, I am confronted
by an absence and forced to reconsider
my more sober faith. I recall how Christ
kept the party at Cana going. How he
commanded others to remember
his body, his blood—the Eucharistic
sacrifice. But what sacrifice could exist
if neither element was not, in some way, joyous?
Once graced with this glimmer of Christ
freed from Gnostic beliefs, I return
to give thanks for the creed
which states that Christ rose
to reign forever, his body restored—
a bright, blood-filled vessel—molded
in the image of the Creator, as are we.

The Priestly Poet

Father Gerard
studies hard.
Wine and bread
are easy to brew
and bake but hell
to transubstantiate.

The poet Hopkins
too modern for Victorians
stores his vision
in metaphor and ink.

Father Gerard
serves his sacrifice. The Word
given life lands lightly on offered
tongues and mine-blackened souls.

The poet Hopkins
sits on pages bound to Whitman
and Yeats, a modern trinity
whose words birthed new generations.

Father Gerard
prays in Latin, mourns
in English; forever racked
by manly doubts, he finds
comfort in ancient rites.

The poet Hopkins
still offers himself to those
who seek their truths
in more secular arts
where printed leaves of dry
black ink can catch fire
and bear witness

to the pied beauty
of golden groves
and human souls.

Gerard and Hopkins
priest and poet,
the perfect partnership
for one might save
what the other had found.

Building Funds

Wake Up the Echoes. . .
—*Notre Dame Fight Song*

In San Benito,
South Texas stops
being North Mexico
on Friday nights.

For noblemen
and peasants alike
the chance to free
souls from purgatory
and to save their own
at any price
seemed a bargain.

In a town poor
for either side
of the border—
where half the kids
drop out—the super-
intendent says
the new stadium,
with its half-million-
dollar scoreboard
and eleven thousand
extra wide seats,
makes perfect sense.

Questionable theology
brought down
the Church
but built
its greatest
basilica.

On Mondays
in classes across
Texas, coaches
teach History
in which indulgence
often repeats itself.

Stroke and Distance—
The Eden Golf and Country Club

Adam made it to 17, a short par 5.
His drive sat square in the middle
of the checker-grained fairway.
His lie was perfect. The Sky Caddie
told him he had 235 left to the green,
215 to the water, 220 to clear the hazard.
As he addressed the ball, preparing
to lay up, a serpent slid between his feet,
coiled around his ball, looked up
and said, *Go for the green. God does.*
Adam stood startled. He had never seen,
let alone named, any species of talking snakes,
but he was even more surprised by the notion
of shooting something other than par.
He never had. There were no handicaps
in paradise. He thought about it
and asked the snake, *Why? Because,*
you can. Adam turned, placed his 7 iron
back
        into the quiver and pulled out a 3 wood.
His heart beat in a rhythm he had never heard.
He muscled up, choked the club's grip.
He sped the tempo of his swing. The extra torque
forced him a bit off-balance. He struck the ball
thin, but, having known only success,
he watched it fly with high hopes until it fell
short, dropped in the drink and kicked up
a terrible spray. Adam reached by reflex
to his hip for an extra ball only to realize
that he wore no pants. The serpent slipped
into the rough and laughed like hell,
while the man stood there dead
certain that he would have to pay
some type of penalty.

Exodus Redux

Del Mar College Library the morning of Hurricane Bret

On five stories of glass,
slaves to the fine print
of our contracts, we labored
to draw giant X
after giant X. Caught
without the blood of lambs,
we settled on using two-inch
masking tape, a modern talisman—
an insane act—a prayer
given up in hopes that the agent
of destruction might pass.

The Theology of Dodge Ball

Capable of great harm
the jock stands armed
on his side of the court
palming a burnt red ball.
Taking aim he hurls a major
league heater at some nerd's
four-eyed head. As if by miracle,
the kid ducks. Surprised
the poor schmuck standing
behind him begins to realize
that he's the next in line.
He can smell the rubber
closing in, can feel his lips
swell before impact, can hear
the spared laugh as he goes
down hard. The same game

gets played each summer
around the gulf—depressions
form into storms, enter deep
liquid heat, pick up steam,
begin to speed and spin.
Coastal rosaries and prayer
chains snap into action. Prayers
go out to the God of mercy
and compassion, to the creator
of all things on heaven and Earth
to steer this dark agent
of destruction onto another path.

Once the barrage ends, the stricken
will be consoled and told that pain's
the price of playing the game.
The spared will heap praise
on a loving God, as a stained ball
slowly rolls back across a gym floor,
while somewhere out in the tropics
a hot sea heaves and swells.

Sins of the Father

Real men—craftsmen
like my father—
can work wonders
with just their hands.

Noah wasn't the most moral
man God could have chosen.
There were others who never drank
nor shed their clothes, but God
knew, for all his faults, Noah
was a real man. With so much riding
on one ark, God knew above all
else, the thing had better float.

Early into any weekend
project, my father
would give me that stare
and the same free advice,
Boy, you better learn
and learn good in school
because you can't do
crap with your hands.

But even in school
they try to teach each boy
how to be a real man.

I nearly failed woodshop
after I failed to lock down
the blade of the power saber
saw, and the simple boot jack
pattern turned into some cubist's
jagged rendition of the great white
shark eating that skinny-dipping
woman in that scene from *Jaws*.

I spent the term sanding
away a desert from its paper
while trying to approximate
an ideal shape. I received a D
from a teacher who didn't
have the nerve to see me repeat.

All ancient history
until tonight as I stand
next to my son during the first
heat of his scout pack's Pinewood
Derby. We will race a boy
blessed with a real father
who has constructed a car
finer than what rolls off
the line at any of the big three.

And so they go, the sins
of one father and the talents
of another, racing each other
down a toy track—
a trial by ordeal
to decide which is more real.

A Father's Confession

Bless me my children for I have sinned
against you. In your infancy,
I often feigned sleep, listened
to your cries until they roused
your mother who would stumble
into her slippers and then stagger
down the hall and into your rooms.

And I have lied to each of you.
Remember when your t-ball coach
yelled to cover third, so you dove
on the base like a GI covering
a hot grenade, how you refused to move
when the kid on the other team tried
to round the corner—that was not a mistake
that everyone makes. Rudolph never ate
the hay you made me place on the roof.
Santa never downed your eggnog.
Bambi's mother was not shot
with a tranquilizing dart and shipped
to a zoo. Goldfish don't sleep belly up,
nor do they vacation in toilet bowls.
I am not sure that fairy godmothers
or guardian angels actually exist.

For my countless outbursts of anger,
for the time you spent fearing my temper,
for the hours I spent ignoring you as I watched
sports, or sat on this worn green couch
filling notebooks with endless drafts
of forgettable poems, for these transgressions
and for all of those that I have left
unsaid, please know that I am heartily sorry.

Know also that I pray the two of you
will thrive, find love, and will someday
learn to forgive your father as I learned
to absolve mine, and he did in kind.

What's Left

               of my father
sits buoyed by pumped oxygen.
He stares across the kitchen table,
past my head and through the faded
and curling wallpaper. We sit
in silence. We never talked
much, but this silence doesn't fit.
It's heavy and woolen. It itches
and constricts, until he says,
Son, I ain't worth a flip. Soon,
I'll need someone to wipe my ass.

Now there's a job that better pay well,
I reply. He brightens, throws me
that look. We laugh, but the silence
begins to lap back in,
                    and sets him adrift.

Psalm of Intentions

God, do you remember that night
my roommate and I waited
for the darkness to take hold
and then drunk on disappointment,
hormones, and a case of Mickey's
Malt Liquor, how we then staggered
up the steep hill on campus to the foot
of the school's ten-story clock tower,
the tower which was lit each night
by spotlights that sat at its base,
and do you remember those boxes
we brought to focus the beams
of the spotlights on our hands,
how the shadows of our fists stood
fifteen feet tall; do you remember
how we counted down from ten
and then lifted our middle fingers,
how we reveled at the thought
of flipping off our dorm, our Catholic
school, the cities of Irving and Dallas,
the distant moon, the universe
and you, God? Do you remember
how it ended when a rent-a-cop yelled,
Hey, you there, how we ran?

God, did you hear us last night
as we, now thirty years older,
sat in a bar, catching up, talking
of our lives, the mess the world
has become? Did you hear us talking
about our dead parents, their dementias
and cancers, the difference between
disappointment and pain? Did you hear
us when we got around to remembering
our school days and our great gesture?

Then God, you must know
that if our anger should ever subside
we might ask for your forgiveness,
but, Father, don't fool yourself,
we knew exactly what we were doing.

The Price of Art

There must be
another planet
in another universe,
one with which God
took his time—a year
or at least a month—
until He got things right,

creating a world
without loss or doubt,
one to which he sent
his only daughter
not to redeem
but to decorate
because in certainty
there is no art.

Divine Error

In a Gnostic Gospel, the child
Christ sits playing, molding clay
into life-sized doves. A young
friend looks on as Christ brings
the birds to his mouth. He breathes
life into the clay. Startled into being,
the doves fly off singing praise.

After a small flock had taken wing,
the child sitting next to Christ snapped.
Unable to take anymore of the Son
of Man's divine showing off, he grabbed
a still clay dove and twisted its head
free from its thin neck and flung
both parts across a small courtyard.
The boy puffed his chest and laughed
as the bird splattered on the hot ground.

Jesus lost control of his human half.
He grabbed his former friend, who felt
the wrath of an angry God pulsing
through him until he, electrified, fell dead.

Mother Mary saw it all. *Jesus
H. Christ! What have you done?*
Jesus didn't have to be omniscient
to know he had stepped into it deep.
Every child understands what it means
when a parent screams a middle name.

By her command and his power,
the playmate was restored. Risen,
the confused boy wept then ran
home where he waited for his chance
to holler and chant, *Crucify him!*
one good Friday in Jerusalem.

Making Sense of Dogma

According to what I'm supposed
to believe, the God who created
the universe, all of that which is seen
and unseen, and sent his only son
to Earth without the benefit
of sex must be some type
of superhero. For as Superman's
powers wilted around kryptonite,
this God cannot beat the chemistry
of the pill or pop a latex rubber—
something that the concussed
and pregnant Lois Lane
can tell you is an easy trick
for the Man of Steel.

The Gospel According to Berecka

If the Gospels are divine missives,
mystically channeled texts
from the Spirit to the saints,
then how did John get
that on part so wrong?

If allowed the chance to edit the canon,
my Jesus would meet Martha on the way
to her brother's tomb. He would tell her
to steady herself and to have faith.
He would teach her, *To everything*
there is a season, and now our dear Lazarus
is but a seed, one that a new orchard
keeper will raise to produce
a fruit sweeter than Eden's apple.

Overcome with grief, she would fail
to understand. In her anger Martha
would banish the Lord, complaining
bitterly to him that this was a time
for action and not empty parables.

After Easter, the risen Christ would travel
with his companion Lazarus, both permanently
raised from the dead. They would visit
the still bereft sisters who would then
understand past all doubt and believe.

But instead, John has Jesus raise Lazarus,
a silent man with a brain starved of oxygen
for four days. John never writes of him again,
the prop in a magic act ushered offstage.
Was the Beloved an experiment in resurrection
gone bad; was he forced to live with a diminished
mind and the stench of death that couldn't be scrubbed

from his once-rotten flesh? Did he ever outlive
his celebrity as the freak—the gimp—
that Jesus brought back from the dead?

But even if Lazarus was restored to his whole
person, why did Jesus—who had preached
that the dead should bury the dead—when
confronted by grief, not find solace in his
Father's plan for his dead friend? Instead
the Lord wept, and his tears fell hard
to earth, and they still shake my core.

Restorations

Jesus, three times larger than life, stands
cast in bronze, erected on marble, balanced
in the bow of a rustic fishing vessel.
He holds his hands out head high, his palms
slightly cupped, his arms outstretched.
His eyes stare past the mad traffic
of Shoreline Drive and out on to the waters
of Corpus Christi Bay, as he calms the waves.

Nothing could calm Santos Rodriguez
that night his love left for good, taking
with her everything, even her scent.
Long sober, Santos stumbled and fell
from the wagon landing hard on a cheap wooden
stool, in a downtown dive where he sat knocking
back bourbon and Cokes, making up
for lost time, until it was too late.

Jesus is not supposed to make mistakes;
it is not in his nature, but the artist
who gave him form had his flaws,
as did the United Methodist who placed
the prized statue so close to the curb
so close to the sharp curve, so Jesus
never saw Santos coming, never took
his fixed gaze away from the waves.

All Santos would recall was wrestling his Beetle
through a thick and self-induced haze, weaving
a drunkard's dance down Shoreline, through the lights
of late-night traffic, and then, as if dreaming,
he was looking up through smoke, steam
and shattered glass at Jesus Christ
whose gigantic arms were held wide
offering Santos a welcoming embrace.

Santos, Santos, Santos... Angels singing?
No, only his mother half grieving, half pleading,
standing next to the hospital bed. Santos
atoned for the pain he had caused,
and proclaimed his gift, a God-given vision,
then he fell back into a deep silent sleep.

Even after Santos learned the truth,
he believed that he had been blessed.
He promised to change his life,
and, to begin this transformation,
he volunteered his time toward the cost
of restoring the damaged art. Accident
or miracle? Who is to know beyond the fact
that for a time and for the same reason,
the bruised Santos and the bronze Jesus
were both in a state of repair.

Good Enough

In every house of my Slavic aunts
and uncles, the same black and white icon
sat tucked in the gilded frames of copies
of *The Last Supper* or a Sacred Heart of Jesus,
in the corners of fading photos of Padre Pio
or Pope Paul—a mass card with a head shot
of the late Catholic president. Too young
in '63, I grew up with no memory of JFK,
yet I was certain he was a modern saint
interred beneath an eternal flame.

But then like George and Christopher,
Saint John F's beatification got torpedoed
by stories of his libido and conquests.
But I confess that as a teen, I was mightily
impressed by knowing that the FBI
had tapes of Marilyn and Jack on his bad back
making the bedsprings sing—a profile
of endurance in deed, and I began
to cherish the tenet that gives each man
the chance to grab for the last rung of purgatory.

Light in Jerusalem

Each year they come on Easter
to the Sepulcher to welcome
the Holy Fire. Pilgrims and the curious
clog the streets encircling the sealed church
in which the Patriarch will pray and wait.

They say he will see the light
seep out of the stone, out
of the tomb. Then like drops
of quicksilver, the glow will gather,
and hover above the holy father
until it sets his candle ablaze—
light from True Light.

They say God's gift might then
enter the street, that the flame
will spread to pilgrim-held candles
and lamps whose wicks will combust
with a fire in which the faithful
can bathe without burning.

Back on duty again this year,
a vigilant and armed Israeli
guard watches for signs
of suicide bombs. By reflex
he sets a cigarette in his lips
and lights it with his Bic.

Easter Art

One young mother broken
by a miscarriage and lost
to therapy was urged to write.
As she healed, her words
formed metaphors, then poems
that fill books and her readers' lives.

Strange that such beauty
should come from a mother's pain.

I knew a mother who sent her boy
out to play. She never understood
the term *freak accident*, never
understood how easily a small skull
could break. She went on with her life,
as if dazed, rarely, if ever, speaking of him
or his death. Self-taught, she began
to paint. Her watercolors and still lifes
fill countless canvasses and the walls
of noted museums and galleries.

Strange that such beauty
should come from a mother's pain.

Mother Mary, who once felt graced,
weeps; her son's broken body rests
heavily upon her, as she questions
how the Father could break
His Word, not yet knowing
how much hope would be found
in her once-borne Word restored.

Strange that so much meaning
has been found in the terrible
beauty of one mother's pain.

Forced Prayer

for Emily

In despair, a mother emailed all she knew,
asking us to pray for the children of Darfur.
She pasted in pictures of those near-ghosts.

Normally unconcerned and never devout,
my first thought is to mark the note as spam,
lest this be the first of many such requests.
But due to our friendship, I reconsider
and begin to calculate the odds that a petition
from someone like me might redirect the attention
of the Omnipotent or teach the Omniscient.

I reread her plea, wince at her expressed guilt
over feeding her own son. I review the images
of the starving. I know she's right. Something
should be done, but not knowing what, I find
myself asking God to send someone else the answer.

Becoming

If a man let himself be lost. . .
—Matthew 16:25

In heaven what will become
of the infirm—those defined
by their disease or syndrome?

Once risen will the elderly
find spring in renewed sinew,
find skin wrinkle-free permanently

pressed? Will the blind, their optic
nerves rewired, see? Will the ungifted
be filled with genius? Will addicts

find a lasting fix? Will schizophrenics
become sane and whole? Will emotions
and social graces visit the autistic?

Will the senile enjoy total recall
of their memories long lost?
Or will we, the so-called normal,

learn that these afflictions were meant
as gifts—the first step into time
squeezed down into the one moment

in which the self, its very presence,
must be erased, atom by atom,
stripped and flayed to its essence—
a simple verb in the I AM's
one true utterance?

Mother Nietzsche: A Modern Pietà

When they changed trains in Frankfurt, she held his dear head,
supporting his chin, once again and kissed his forehead. It was all
over for Nietzsche.
                    —Ronald Hayman, *Nietzsche: A Critical Life*

Mother Nietzsche weeps.
Her son's mind, lost to reason,
rests on her thigh. Their compartment
is empty with well-wishers
and filled only with the sounds
of their locomotion and his eyes.

The spent Christ carved in white—
found in stone by the seeker
Michelangelo—rests on Mary,
consumed by love and grief, who
holds no hope for what the stone
knows and is now ours to doubt.

Mother Nietzsche weeps for
she has no doubts. A minister's
wife, she knows Zarathustra
will not rise. She avoids his eyes—
eyes that have seen too far,
past everything and on to nothing
where the truth cannot hide.

His courage, her fear still remain
uncarved, not for the want of skill
or hand, but for the want of a proper stone.
For a stone so hard and so black
could never hold another form
but must collapse into the infinite
density of the seeker's final vision.

The Visit

Long cured from Catholic church-
going, we're surprised when a lady
from our old parish calls. The Legion
of Mary wants to offer us the chance
to bring the Virgin home and pray
the rosary at her as a family;
we can each name our own special
intention, no donation required.

My wife begins to do some world class
backpedaling. She's tactfully lobbing
excuses like empty oil drums at the legion's
feet, but these are tough commandos—
part ninja, part nun. They keep coming.

I ask my exasperated spouse for a chance
to speak with the legionnaire. Since I always
avoid telephones, my request stuns her,
but I'm feeling a certain calling, so I ask again.
She stands there frozen as if she half-expects
a flaming tongue to appear and hover above
my head as I grab the drooping receiver.

I introduce myself and say hello.
I ask the church lady on the other end
if we would have to bring the Queen
of Heaven straight home. I'm thinking
that the poor saint might be tiring
of spending all her time listening
to the same series of prayers muttered
by poor souls looking to find divine favor.
I'm thinking, *What about Mary?*
Perhaps, we could take her to a salon,
buy her a makeover or at least a pedicure.
Then we could make a night of it,

go out for a meal, drink some Blue Nun,
or Saint Pauli Girls, tell a few jokes,
have a few laughs, then go catch a chick flick
unless she'd rather play Putt-Putt or roll a few frames.
As my wife throws me a zealot's stare,
the phone goes dead without a word
as if disconnected by a prayer.

But I'm feeling a little disappointed.
I can't help picturing Mary as a girl
way before that angel showed up.
She must have played, made plans,
enjoyed life and the mundane, back
when being human seemed enough.

Shopping for Miracles: Lourdes, 1979

Looking for a cheap souvenir, I browsed
the curio shops. Deciding against frisbees
stamped with Mary or t-shirts picturing
the sainted Bernadette, I opted
for a convertible virgin, a plastic bottle
with a threaded neck and screw-top head.
Pleased with the absurdity of my purchase,
I walked to the shrine, past the grotto
and its glass-encased stream. I waded
through the tides of the sick and dying
to a brass tap where I filled my Mary
to her Adam's apple—half hoping the water
might cure my bed-bound mother.

Exiting the grounds, I passed bazooka-sized
votives and eyed the infirm. I noticed
that the ill seemed to suffer most from aging.
Confused, I began to question our shared faith—
*Everyone wants to meet Jesus, but nobody
wants to die*—the old adage come to life. I grew
tired to my marrow. I saw a rusted garbage bin
and decided to can my plastic Queen of Heaven,
but when I lifted the tin lid, there on top
of the trash sat a broken wooden cane.

I returned to the States with a glass flask
filled with holy water which I gave
to my mother who accepted the gift
with gratitude, although she remained
bedridden and continued to say the rosary
through her pain every day until she died.

The American Cathedral

Young Staples aspired to fame and piety,
to become the American Padre Pio.
He too would dress in brown woolen robes,
and, God willing, he would learn to hear
silent confessions, hover above the altar
during high mass, allow his spirit to travel
as he slept to comfort souls darkened by doubt,
but mostly he wished to heal the sick with hands
that God would pierce with fragrant wounds.

But his years in the pulpit only brought
Young Staples to middle age, so he decided
to trade in Jesus Christ for Adam Smith,
Catholicism for capitalism, middlemen
for buying wholesale-direct. He renounced
his vows and fell in bed then love with an earthy
woman. He began to preach a new brand
of Good News. Each Sunday he promises his flock
everything in glossy ads found between the comics
and the classifieds, and his disciples come
in great numbers, believing that their problems
can be solved by shopping in the city
of Corpus Christi at the Padre Staples Mall.

Why Theology and Economics Don't Mix

As soon as we got back to the car
our father always asked, *So what'chya get?*
Meaning we better produce something
pilfered from the just-visited restaurant.
Doggy bags didn't count, but a shrimp fork,
or juice glass, spoon, napkin, or if nothing
else, packs of sugar or crackers would do.

My mother never played along.
She voiced her disgust, to which dad
replied, *Ah nuts! It defrays the cost.*

I hadn't thought about these petty
thefts for years. Then this Sunday
at mass, the priest preached on the text
about how the apostles met a stranger
on the road to Emmaus. How they invited
the man to dine with them, and how
it wasn't until the bread had been broken
and the stranger disappeared that they
recognized the Lord. And I began to wonder
just how often Jesus had skipped out on the check.

Flashes

I

Mom! Our fear rose, climbed the cellar stairs
with the smell of ozone and scorched metal.

She sought peace, sent us down
to the basement of a house built
too small for kids on a rain-soaked day.

My older sister told me to help
set up an old metal table. She planned
to draw pictures. We flipped it on its back
and worked together to raise a stubborn leg.
Then needing a rest, we stepped back.

Lightning found the leg eight feet underground
through a window the size of a cinder block.

Mom considered the odds of the strike.
She added in the fact that her kids
weren't hurt. The math froze her halfway
down the stairs. We charged her.

My sister and I spent the afternoon
coloring at our wooden kitchen table.
We strained to keep our crayons
within the lines as each thunder
clap echoed in our hearts.

II

My cousin Adam—never a genius
nor a fan of adages—managed
to get struck by lightning twice.
Both times as he drove his Ford
tractor through a hayfield, towing
a kick-baler, hoping to get in

one more load before it stormed.
Both times he was knocked out
and clear off the tractor. He came to
drenched, numb and wondering
where the hell his Ford had gone.

My grandmother claimed that back
in the old country, back before
the one true faith took root,
the pagans believed Perkunas,
the God of Thunder, chose his priests
by testing them with his power.
Those who survived a lightning
strike were said to be touched by God.
She did not know what it meant
to be twice called. My father concluded,
That damn idiot must be really touched.

III
Certain tragedies border on the slapstick.
A part of me wants to laugh when I think
of Thomas Merton as he stepped
from his Thai shower, stood
in a dripped pool of water
and turned on that shorted fan,
or that preacher in Waco who brought
an ungrounded mike into a baptismal pool.

Both met the power
no man can survive—
the sudden convergence
of heat and light,
a collect call from God
or perhaps just a current
jumping its course,
to find a saint or fool,
or the two fused in kind.

Throwing the Morning News

3 a.m. seemed always the same, for at 3 a.m.
middle class neighborhoods have no life.
But once, the time came on a night
when clouds and calendars ate all natural
light leaving the streets darker than

Nijinsky's heart that last time
he stood on stage and told his confused
audience that his dance was not for their
diversion, that his art was too subtle
for those who could forget about the trenches
that filled with human blood and corpses.

In this darkness I turned from Nightingale
on to Kingfisher when my lights beaming
low, caught two blocks of taillights, grills,
bumpers, reflectors, hydrant markers,
and stray cats' eyes. Jewels of light—
the spectrum given life—danced,
filling empty space. The creation
stunned me, and I stopped
                              but not for long.

The night's mindless tasks busied my hands,
but my mind could not shake free
from that instance of light. I thought of creations
and creators. My schoolbook theology
began to stretch, then tore. I wondered
if God is ever surprised by a poet's
phrase, a dancer's turn. I started to believe
that art serves to reveal to man his divinity
and remind the Divine of His omnipotence.

The Sacrament of Marriage
for BJ and Rachael

After the vows are said and the rings
exchanged, know that there will be bad
neighbors who will fill your backyard
with spent beer bottles and disturb
your life with their noise and stereos.

There will be the boring and soul-
numbing jobs that you will stay in
for the health insurance and the assurance
that the bills will be paid, and the kids
will have what they need
and some of what they want.

There will be short hot arguments
where things that should never
be said will be shouted and screamed.

There will be the small peeves—
drawers left open, seats left up,
the hot curling iron left
in the way of the toothpaste.

There's always a price
for the quiet moment,
the stolen kiss, the cold nights
spent teaspooned together—
those near miraculous moments
when should you be asked
if you still believed that life
was worth it, you'd answer

without thinking, *I do.*

On the Night of Our 20th Anniversary
for Alice

Poets often write about lying awake
surrounded by the history of their homes.
They recall uncovered clues: pencil marks
on doorjambs, spackled scars on walls,
photographs found in attics and closets.
From these remnants, the poets surmise
the lives of past residents and write
their poems which will bless or pass judgment
on the long-gone keepers of their shared space.

This night, unable to sleep myself,
I listen to my wife's heavy breaths.
While braced for the occasional snore,
I come to realize that I can abide
this two-story house, despite
its sinking foundation, the spots
of dry rot and peeling paint. Still,
I am not drawn to conjecture about
the old judge and his wife who built
this place. Instead, my mind falls
back into a one-room cinder block
apartment, once set whirling
by an eddy of passion that spun
us together and then together again
and again, until we loved each other
raw and fell asleep shoehorned
into a sagging twin bed.

Blistered feet will heal once leather
shoes get broken in. Tonight we lie
on our adjustable queen-sized air bed.
I keep my half much softer than hers.
We each have found a certain level
of comfort. She rolls onto her side.

The room goes silent. I figure only a poet
might someday buy a house as broken
down as this. When that moving day
comes, I plan to leave an old pair of wing
tips in our bedroom closet, so some night
a young poet might lie here and glean
the truth about this love that we now share.

The Value of Salt

You are the salt.
          —Matthew 5:13

My father covered his t-bones and fries
in blizzards of salt. He insisted
that I try it, forcing me to shake
a dusting onto my food. He claimed
the seasoning brought out hidden flavors,
but all I could ever taste was salt.

In the winter he carried a torn bag
of rock salt. Like a farmer feeding
chickens, he scattered handfuls
to melt the iced walk that led
to a rusted Rambler. He drove us
into the city on a bed of salted sand,

to early mass at Saint George's
where a stern friar stared down
from the pulpit, warned his flock
not to become salt that lost its flavor,
while I gave thanks for my father's diet—
the long odds of salt ever being bland—
and sensed the hint of God's savor.

Zen and the Art of Metaphysical Maintenance— On First Reading Persig

All of the philosophers he was reading showed it. The whole university he was attending smelled of the same ugliness. It was everywhere, in the classroom, in the textbooks. It was in himself and he didn't know how or why. It was reason itself that was ugly and there seemed no way to get free.
      —Robert Persig, Zen and the Art of Motorcycle Maintenance

Fixed, I stare
at hand and wrist—
one must end
the other begins
but where? Two days
out, this simple problem
drowns me. I read
scars and lines, discover
faint hairs, log shades
of autumn maples
and sky all found
deep in white skin.
Friends voice concern—
*Something needs to be
done.* I drink Scotch
neat. My mind given
over to visions, spins on—
it sees every page
of every book I ever
read, I watch cheap ball-
points refill pads with notes
for classes long passed—
I retake exams, relive
conversations—six days
in, I stare on but add ice
to Johnny Walker—its label
red as blood—my body
can't keep up—the brain speeds—

racing back past the stem
to its roots—ransacking
its way to the primal
cause—the first cog
that turned the machine.
Logic turns brittle—
Snaps—the universe
as syllogism explodes—
the Big Bang
between the ears—
good God—what's left—
passion and fear—
as if something
like love might
stand behind
it all.

this sentence.
beyond
that waits
and grace
of mercy
a glimpse
hem and catch
the tattered
of grazing
in hopes
reaching up
stretching,
and stand
their balance
might find
which some
rows, on
into mortared
the remains
stacking
the rubble
work sifting
where poets
into lexicons
that fell
language
created
The Word

The Tower

Alan Berecka is an accidental poet. Raised in rural New York, his boyhood introduction to poetry occurred during an NFL halftime show which featured Kipling's *If* set to highlights. As an English major at the University of Dallas, he studied the poetry of D. H. Lawrence and Gerard Manley Hopkins. After graduating, he worked as a telephone operator. Two years of arguing over quarters made him nostalgic for academia, so he entered graduate school at the University of North Texas. While there a graduate level creative writing class was offered. He took the class in hopes that he would be told to quit writing poetry. His plan backfired. Berecka ended up winning the University's poetry contest, and Rick Sale advised Berecka to write a creative thesis. He graduated with an MA in Interdisciplinary Studies. While at UNT, Alan met Alice Adams, and the two married and started a family. Upon graduating the only work the new father could find was throwing a paper route, so he entered Texas Woman's University and earned an MLS. Later, as a librarian, Berecka wrote little and submitted even less. And then eight years into his career, while working at McLennan Community College in Waco, Dana Gioia came to the school to read. By chance Berecka was assigned to drive Gioia. During those drives, they conversed about Elizabeth Bishop and poetry in general. Gioia encouraged Berecka to attend the West Chester Poetry Conference and wrote letters to a reluctant Berecka encouraging him to return his application. Berecka, conflicted about this possible return to poetry, went to see Fr. Bill Carroll, who lectured his parishioner on the parable of talents. Later that year, Berecka attended Mark Jarman's narrative workshop. His rekindled desire to write has enriched his life and brought him many friendships.He and Alice now live in Sinton, TX, where they raised their children, Rachael and Aaron. Berecka earns his keep as reference librarian at Del Mar College in Corpus Christi, TX. Author's web site: www.alanberecka.com

www.ingramcontent.com/pod-product-compliance
Lightning Source LLC
Chambersburg PA
CBHW071234090426
42736CB00014B/3072